JOHN BETJEMAN

Greg Morse

SHIRE PUBLICATIONS

Published in Great Britain in 2011 by Shire Publications Ltd, Midland House, West Way, Botley, Oxford OX2 0PH, UK.

44-02 23rd Street, Suite 219, Long Island City, NY 11101, USA.

E-mail: shire@shirebooks.co.uk   www.shirebooks.co.uk

A CIP catalogue record for this book is available from the British Library.

Shire Library no. 648.   ISBN-13: 978 0 74781 051 3

Greg Morse has asserted his right under the Copyright, Designs and Patents Act, 1988, to be identified as the author of this book.

Designed by Tony Truscott Designs, Sussex, UK and typeset in Perpetua and Gill Sans.
Printed in China through Worldprint Ltd.

11 12 13 14 15   10 9 8 7 6 5 4 3 2 1

COVER IMAGE
A pensive John Betjeman sitting on a train, 1959.

TITLE PAGE IMAGE
John Betjeman, the most popular Poet Laureate since Tennyson, waits on a London Underground platform in characteristic mirthful pose, 31 January 1974.

CONTENTS PAGE IMAGE
Magdalen College, Oxford, represented freedom when Betjeman went there in 1925. This vintage postcard view shows the quad much as it looked at the height of the rivalry between the artistic 'aesthetes' and the sporty 'hearties'.

ACKNOWLEDGEMENTS
I am indebted to Julia Jenkins, Roger Badger, Kathryn Badger, Loreen Brown (Hodder), Paul Chancellor (Colour-Rail), Bevis Hillier, Cassie Metcalf-Slovo (Aitken Alexander), John R. Murray, Virginia Murray, Gavin Stamp and Mary Ann Sullivan for their kindness and assistance throughout the writing of this book. Especial thanks are due to my very good friends David Brown and John Heald (Vice-Chairman, The Betjeman Society) for their proofreading skills and expert advice. Finally, I thank Nick Wright, Emily Brand and Russell Butcher at Shire Publications for making my first foray with them such an enjoyable experience.

I would also like to thank the people who have allowed me to use illustrations, which are acknowledged as follows: Roger Badger, pages 19, 34, 39, 42 (bottom) and 52; British Rail, page 35; Colour-Rail/Paul Riley, page 32 (bottom); Getty Images, cover and page 1; The Hon. Mrs Derek Jackson, page 6; Julia Jenkins, page 45; Sir Osbert and Lady Lancaster, page 11; London Transport Museum, page 20; Chris McEvoy, page 51; John Murray Archive, pages 8, 9, 25, 38, 40 and 48; National Railway Museum/SSPL, page 28; Gavin Stamp, page 46; M. A. Sullivan, page 13.

Shire Publications is supporting the Woodland Trust, the UK's leading woodland conservation charity, by funding the dedication of trees.

CONTENTS

INTRODUCTION

FROM THE GLOOM of the booking office shuffles a shadowy figure. Sporting a Pickwickian hat and a long mac misshapen by maps and guidebooks, he peers into the distance as a steam train bound for Somewhere-on-sea hoves into view. Turning, he smiles crookedly at the television camera and delivers a perfect prose-poem commentary on the scene, which we are, I fear, about to witness for the last time. The year is 1963; the man, of course, is John Betjeman.

By the early 1960s Betjeman had gained recognition as a best-selling poet, writer and broadcaster with a cause. 'If I have a mission,' he told a journalist in 1955, 'it is to show people things which are beautiful so that they will very soon realise what is ugly. When you look *at* things, instead of just looking through them, life starts absolutely crackling with interest and excitement.' Critical of post-war social trends, government policy and building practices, he did indeed do much to help us appreciate beauty in the landscape, in architecture, in churches, on the coast – and on the railway.

As fellow poet Philip Larkin observed, Betjeman's marriage of people and place created a new kind of poetry. The novelist Kingsley Amis added that the verses sometimes challenged the reader unexpectedly, so that often the message was: 'in the midst of life, we're in death.' Set in London's private medical district, 'Devonshire Street W.1' (1953) provides an example, contrasting the heavy door of a doctor's rooms with the heavy heart of his terminally ill patient, and connecting the cold iron of the palisade with the uncaring world that carries on regardless of the man, his wife and their life together.

And yet Betjeman has been labelled rather unflatteringly as a 'teddy bear to the nation'. For many, this describes perfectly the unthreatening pillar of the establishment that the creator of 'fair Elaine' and 'Miss Joan Hunter Dunn' seemed to become. The image was heightened by his interest in tennis-playing blonde 'gels', like the Amazonian Pam of 'Pot Pourri from a Surrey Garden' (1938), and by Archibald, his teddy bear.

In fact, the carrying of that fluffy toy from tutorial to tutorial was a deliberate gesture of defiance during the poet's Oxford undergraduate days in the 1920s. But by the 1980s the idea of a grown man keeping a stuffed bear on his pillow was enough to fill some critics with laughter. Most of the lords and ladies of academia laughed so hard they forgot to write about him. Alas, Betjeman's 'cuddly' façade and the apparently endless stream of stories about his personal life detract from his work, which remains moving – and relevant. Consider the 'Executive', who first appeared in 1971. Today's white-collar wanderer may drive something more modern than the 'firm's Cortina', but he still spouts jargon and still has scant regard for anything over five years old. A present-day version of Browning's materialist Duke (cf. 'My Last Duchess', 1842), he therefore reaches back some one hundred years *and* looks forward to twenty-first-century consumerism.

Crucially, 'Executive' confirms Betjeman to have had the original mind that the Oxford don Maurice Bowra recognised; it was an originality that allowed him to reflect the era through which he lived and to connect with the lives of his many readers in many ways. This book explores some of them.

Although Betjeman's first volume of poetry was published in 1931 by the artist and patron Edward James, it would be another Oxford friend, John Murray, who became the central figure in presenting his work to the world. The famous publishing house, based here at 50 Albemarle Street W1 until 2002, has also counted Byron and Jane Austen among its authors.

BECOMING THE POET

I N A STREET just off Hampstead Heath, not far from Gospel Oak station on the North London Line, stands a row of red Victorian flats. The Lissenden Gardens estate was built at the end of the nineteenth century. Its architects, Boehmer and Gibbs, had incorporated a number of 'Arts and Crafts' signatures into their work, such as hand-made red clay roof tiles, hand-tapered bricks on the arches over the windows, and wrought-iron detailing. This loose link with William Morris would be galvanised in the years ahead by the child born in no. 52 Parliament Hill Mansions on 28 August 1906: John Betjemann, future journalist, broadcaster, preservationist, and the most popular Poet Laureate since Alfred, Lord Tennyson.

At this stage, the family was using the double 'n' version of its name, which had been adopted during the mania for Germany inspired by Queen Victoria's marriage to Prince Albert of Saxe-Coburg and Gotha. Despite later assertions about their supposed Dutch origins, the Betjemanns *were* German, the family having arrived in London during the late eighteenth century. At the time of his son's birth, Ernest Betjemann was, like the two generations before him, working for the family firm, G. Betjemann & Sons, cabinet makers and silversmiths of Pentonville Road. The company was best known for the invention of the tantalus — a small spirit stand that allowed decanters to be locked in place to prevent theft. Ernest was a devotee of hunting, shooting and fishing, and hoped John would follow him both in these manly pursuits and (eventually) in his career. But the child had other interests, as the adult would reflect in his verse-autobiography, *Summoned by Bells* (1960):

> I knew as soon as I could read and write
> That I must be a poet ...

At first, Ernest encouraged his son, buying him books, reading poetry to him and organising trips to the Tate Gallery. During one such visit, they came upon Frank Bramley's *A Hopeless Dawn* (1888), a moving picture in which a young woman weeps into her mother-in-law's lap as she realises that her

Opposite: Pamela Mitford captioned this photograph 'Betch ready for London on Monday morning'. He was heading for the offices of the *Architectural Review*, the staff of which he joined in 1930.

husband is lost at sea. John was captivated, but it was Ernest who urged him to paint a similar picture in verse, even suggesting the opening couplet. John's attempt caused embarrassment when he looked back on it in 1960, but it showed how the desire to write was becoming important.

John's mother, Mabel (known as 'Bess'), was the daughter of an artificial-flower manufacturer from Highbury. She tends to be portrayed as a slightly silly hypochondriac, but she was also a suffragette who attended Mrs Pankhurst's meetings, and whom Betjeman would later ask to summarise novels for his review column in the *Daily Herald*. When adolescence turned paternal love into 'black waves of hate', it was to his mother that the growing boy would cling.

Betjeman was born into a middle-class world of Cornish holidays, nannies and nursery-maids, awash with mid-Edwardian class-consciousness. This was something that affected him all his life and shaped his desire to scale the social ladder. The family move to an elegant Highgate villa, 31 West Hill, in 1909 was part of such a climb. It was here that John met Peggy Purey-Cust, the perfect blue-eyed daughter of an admiral, who set the standard against which he measured all other women for many years. She was the child who, in his poet's mind, grew into countless tennis-playing, khaki-wearing sports girls.

Betjeman always professed deep love for 31 West Hill, but it was not all trains, teddy bears and buttered toast. Sadly, where there are schoolboys, there are often bullies and the future Laureate found himself a target when the fashion for 'all things German' was replaced by fear during the First World War:

> Betjemann's a German spy –
> Shoot him down and let him die:
> Betjemann's a German spy,
> A German spy, a German spy!

In practice, shooting was replaced by smashing windows – as happened to a local German baker – and by kicking and punching, as happened to the young John. On one occasion, two boys enticed him from his usual route home with false promises of kindness, only to strip him of his shorts and push him into a prickly holly bush. He would drop the double 'n' (as his mother had done during the War) around 1922, but sanctuary was sought first in books – and in writing poetry. One master at Highgate Junior School, which John attended at this time, was proudly given a handwritten volume entitled *The Best of Betjeman*. His name was T. S. Eliot.

Betjeman's happy childhood home, 31 West Hill, Highgate, is on the right of this 1909 photograph, which shows his neighbour Ethelwynne Bouman (and her daughter Betty) outside no. 30.

It was also probably at Highgate Junior that Betjeman first read Tennyson and the *Golden Treasury*, an anthology of English poetry selected by Francis Turner Palgrave in 1861, and which featured Coleridge, William Cowper, Keats, Pope and Wordsworth. It was to have a profound influence on his writing and was so beloved that he named it as the book choice for his second appearance on BBC Radio's *Desert Island Discs* in 1975.

In 1917, at the age of nine, Betjeman was sent to the Dragon School in Oxford, where he boarded for three years. Here his interest in poetry grew and his acting and oration skills started to flourish. One favourite schoolmaster, Gerald Haynes, also helped shape John's future by encouraging the study of churches and botany. Indeed, it was now that the poet's penchant for 'church crawling' – and for architecture in general – began to take form.

The family continued to climb socially and, when John returned home during the holidays, he found that they had moved to Chelsea. Now his mother could boast loose connections (via friends of friends of friends) with the artist Augustus John. But Betjeman was becoming more interested in architecture than painting, his original preference being for Georgian buildings, whose beauty and proportion pleased his aesthetic sensibilities.

Marlborough College

Hont's Studio
Marlboro.

The entrance to
Marlborough
College, c. 1920.

Where poetry was concerned, however, he was starting to align himself with
the later nineteenth century. This became evident at Marlborough College,
to which he progressed in 1920, and at which he presented a scathing
paper to the College Literary Society on second-rate *early* Victorian
writing. More seriously, he became interested in Swinburne and fellow
Marlburian William Morris; he also began to read, quote and correspond
with Lord Alfred Douglas.

And yet Marlborough was repressive, and he would often spend time
alone reflecting and dreaming in the college chapel. There were bullies here
too, in the form of prefects who had the power to beat students and inflict
all manner of torments and punishments on those who did not comply. After
this stifling regime, Oxford University represented freedom on a grand scale.
As one might expect, he cut tutorials, drank too much and began to dress as
he liked (which for him meant silk ties, handkerchiefs and other 'foppish'
ephemera). Here, he met many people, such as the future *Daily Express*
cartoonist Osbert Lancaster, who would be his friends for life. He also met
W. H. Auden, who entered Christ Church in 1925, the same year Betjeman
went up to Magdalen. Both men would eventually study English, but the
Oxford English school syllabus in those days ended with the Romantics.
Betjeman's tutor, one C. S. Lewis, was unsympathetic to the call of Victorian
verse, and unsympathetic to Betjeman; the young undergraduate was thus
left to his own devices (and those of friends like the Dean of Wadham,
Maurice Bowra, and the University Lecturer in Spanish, G. A. Kolkhorst) to

discover the delights of Thomas Hardy, and rediscover Tennyson, for himself. It would be poets like these who would be reflected, revered and remembered in his own work.

At the end of *Summoned by Bells*, Betjeman is sent down from Oxford for failing his Divinity examination and is left with nothing but a huge bill at Blackwell's bookshop and great pressure to find himself a job. In fact, he did not fail this exam, but obtained a pass degree. The problem was that pass degrees are aimed more at sporty types than arty types, so – to him – he might as well have failed, particularly as this would not have been enough to let him become a don, seeking out obscure poets in the Bodleian Library and solace in the college chapel.

Unable to bring himself to fulfil his father's wish by working for the family firm, he went instead to a scholastic agency in Sackville Street to seek employment as a schoolmaster. It was to be an occupation he enjoyed twice: once at Gerrards Cross, and then again (after a brief spell as Private Secretary to the Irish agricultural reformer Sir Horace Plunkett) at Heddon Court Preparatory School in Barnet. The novelist Evelyn Waugh told him that he would remember 'these school days' as the happiest of his life. Betjeman later likened them to a regular 'solo turn' on the music-hall circuit. It doubtless helped prepare him for the many performances which lay ahead; but this malaise was not to last, for the following decade would see him become a professional writer. In brief, he started work for the *Architectural Review* (1930), published an ardent account of architectural styles (*Ghastly Good Taste*, 1933) and a book on the University of Oxford (*An Oxford University Chest*, 1938). He also conceived the *Shell Guides* (1932) and wrote film reviews for the *Evening Standard* between 1934 and 1935. Most significantly, in 1931, the artist and patron Edward James announced his intention to publish his old Oxford friend's poetry. The two delighted in discussing which obscure typefaces and what sort of paper might be used to show the work off to good effect.

The cover of the resulting volume, *Mount Zion (or In Touch with the Infinite)* (1931), sported an engraving of a wasp-waisted woman on the telephone. The contents were printed on coloured bond; the binding featured the type of paper used for indoor fireworks. Betjeman's interest in book design threatened to overshadow the contents, and yet the opening poem, 'Death in Leamington', is as perfect a marriage of people and place as he would ever manage. It was a clear sign of what was to come.

The cover art for Betjeman's first volume of poetry, *Mount Zion (or In Touch with the Infinite)*, published by Edward James in 1931.

MOUNT ZION

OR

IN TOUCH WITH THE INFINITE

BETJEMAN AND ARCHITECTURE

A S BETJEMAN talked on the telephone to Pamela Mitford, he could not help noticing that the office was slowly filling with photographs of caves and rock-carvings, which the woman kneeling on the floor wanted to use to illustrate her article on Indian art. Finishing his conversation, he joined her to help make the most appropriate selection. She – Penelope Chetwode, daughter of the Commander in Chief in India – knew that he, assistant editor of the *Architectural Review*, was not particularly interested in her subject. But he certainly liked what he saw. The two fell in love and were married in 1933. They would later have two children, Paul and Candida.

Betjeman reflected that he left the *Architectural Review* because he needed more money, but he was already starting to drift away from its editorial policy. Joining the magazine in October 1930, he had found himself in a maelstrom of Modernism – a path he too would follow for a while, writing in various styles under various pseudonyms (like Lionel Cuffe and – probably – Rockingham Newbolt). We are used to Betjeman as the protector of all things Victorian – from Gilbert Scott's St Pancras station hotel in London to the elegant ironwork of Clevedon Pier in Somerset. So how did this apparent aberration come about?

The '*Archie Rev*' (as Betjeman christened it) was edited by Christian Barman, but its owner, Hubert de Cronin Hastings, had the real power and was not above telephoning abrupt orders to the *Review*'s offices in Queen Anne's Gate from various holiday hideaways. Both Hastings and his principal writer, Philip Morton Shand, were evangelists for the radical Modern Movement, which held that traditionalism was a bar to human progress. In architectural terms, this largely meant lavishing praise on the Swiss-French architect Le Corbusier and Walter Gropius's Bauhaus school. Betjeman may have found this more appealing than the 'phoney' mainstream architecture of the day, but his genuine opinion had to grapple with his desire to subvert, his need to be funny and the expectation that he toe the editorial line (at least to an extent). While Hastings certainly indulged Betjeman, he remained more than happy to guide him in his own inimitable way if he felt it necessary.

Writing about a forthcoming article by his young protégé, for example, he explained that 'what Mr John Betjeman calls the "Awf'lly Modern Movement"' was in fact 'a mocking reference to Art Deco' (which Hastings hated) and not to the Modern Movement proper. This sort of 'guidance' accounts for the rather awkward connections Betjeman then makes between the neo-classicist Bank of England architect Sir John Soane and Modernism, amid his survey of Victorian decorative arts.

Betjeman had begun to explore nineteenth-century aesthetics at the Dragon School, buying a book of late-Victorian watercolours, whose images of Oxford were so captivating that they could still blot out the city's noisy reality when he was writing *Summoned by Bells* some forty years later. By the time he reached Marlborough College in 1920, however, he had started to laugh at Victorian buildings (although, as an adolescent, he doubtless found *everything* funny). At Magdalen, five years later, the lure of the Gothic style had waned and was replaced in his affections by Georgian architecture. The love of this period was evident in his 1938 book *An Oxford University Chest*, with its painterly description of St Ebbes, and in a 1963 television film, which

When Betjeman joined the staff of the *Architectural Review* in 1930, the Modern Movement was much in vogue. One of its chief exponents was the Swiss-French architect Le Corbusier. The embodiment of Le Corbusier's ideas was Villa Savoye, the concrete country house he built at Poissy, near Paris.

saw him take a dual role, arguing with himself as a developer who wanted to raze 'Georgeean' Bath to the ground.

Betjeman retained his interest in this era, but if he wanted to show his sneaking regard for later nineteenth-century styles at the '*Archie Rev*', he had to employ subtle tactics. On one occasion, he managed to persuade the Arts and Crafts architect C. F. A. Voysey to make a contribution. Voysey wrote in praise of Gothic, which he felt to be a practical principle that did not necessarily depend on imitating 'familiar Gothic detail' like pointed arches and ribbed vaults. For Voysey, the Great Exhibition of 1851 'awakened the idea of unity as the basis of Art'. 'All that was necessary for daily life,' he went on, 'could be, and ought to be, made beautiful' – a very Arts and Crafts sentiment indeed. Pugin (remembered for his work on the Palace of Westminster) had designed the Exhibition's Medieval Court, so it was clearly a Gothic high point. Linking all this together allowed Betjeman to suggest that the emphasis on 'necessity' marked a return to 'simplicity' from 'the complex and futile revivalism in which many architects still remain'. By adding that this process had already begun on the Continent, he managed to get away with it.

The confusion Betjeman felt at this time was reflected in his book *Ghastly Good Taste* (1933), which discussed the effects of industrialisation on architecture and was clearly aligned to the Hastings–Shand axis. Even William Morris, a Betjeman favourite alongside Voysey, does not escape criticism.

The Gothic splendour of the Palace of Westminster, c. 1945. The architect was Sir Charles Barry; interior detail was by Pugin.

THE PALACE OF WESTMINSTER, LONDON H 699

Feeling contrite when writing a new preface in 1970, he said that he was 'appalled' by the book's 'sententiousness, arrogance and sweeping generalisations'. The lack of sympathy in its pages is somewhat at odds with the tone of his contemporary poems (like 'Death in Leamington' and 'For Nineteenth Century Burials'), but *Ghastly Good Taste* is theoretical, and Betjeman is always at his best when he can see people. This is particularly apparent in his article on Leeds (also published in 1933).

'To understand Leeds,' he wrote, 'one must acquire a Leeds sense of proportion.' This could be achieved by realising that Leeds is a parochial Victorian city, two qualities that are 'far more blessed than is generally supposed.' From the 'large, gas-lit stations' out into the 'industrialised communities', Betjeman is both romantic and realistic. So, Brodrick's Town Hall of 1858 is 'fine', and the nineteenth-century warehouses and mills are 'the cathedrals of the industrial north'. Appraising the 'appalling' slum housing, he added: 'I think a city which has such remarkable people should take better care of them.'

Betjeman's openness and maturity, later nurtured by the artist John Piper (with whom he collaborated on various guide books), was reflected in 1961 when he wrote in praise of Park Hill, a modern block of flats in Sheffield. One would expect such a building to be loathed by a man who would refer to the 'rent-collecting slabs' by Hyde Park in a speech the following year, and later still would write about the 'arid, monotonous new cubes with their

Vintage postcard of Brodrick's Town Hall, Leeds. Betjeman was impressed by the 1858 building when he visited the city in 1933 for the *Architectural Review*.

Town Hall, Leeds.

garish mosaics' in London's Gresham Street. Park Hill might have suffered from ugly detailing, but even if 'you cannot make out which dot in the area below is your child, you are at least centrally heated and with hot water and proper sanitation'. He clearly recognised that this was by no means the *best* solution to the slum problem, but it was better than the modern suburb he found in the city, where there seemed to be no shops ('only houses, houses'), and which seemed to be 'a wasteful use of Sheffield's countryside'.

The outbreak of war in 1939 marked something of a watershed for Betjeman. Many of the poems in his subsequent volume of verse, *Old Lights for New Chancels* (1940), represent his own attempt 'to catch the atmosphere of places and times' in his homeland. Thus we have a celebration of 'Cheltenham', from which we travel north via the old Midland Railway to meet 'A Shropshire Lad'. Although this poem gestures ironically towards A. E. Housman's well-known work, and although the note that it should be 'recited with a Midland accent' is undoubtedly teasing, the description is at least as sympathetic as that which Betjeman had used in his article on Leeds:

> The sun was low on the railway line
> And over the bricks and stacks,
> And in at the upstairs windows
> Of the Dawley houses' backs.

Much of Betjeman's wartime prose and radio broadcasts also celebrated Britain, placing greater emphasis on encouraging people to look about them. This was vital both in easing the anxieties of those who were unable to fight on the front line and in highlighting what was being fought for.

The Butter Cross at Ludlow in the early 1960s. Built in 1744, this elegant stone structure was the Shropshire town's butter market. Betjeman paid a visit while working with John Piper on a guide to the county in the 1940s.

The Circus at Bath in the 1950s. This postcard portrays the pre-shot-blasted Bath, as featured in Betjeman's 1963 television film on the city.

And yet an even bigger threat than the German bombers – in Betjeman's eyes – was on the horizon. His poem 'The Planster's Vision' (1945) highlights the blatant disregard for the past that he feared would taint post-war Britain. This 'vision of the future' is revisited in 'The Town Clerk's Views' (1958), where the Clerk himself hopes to blight the country with soulless concrete villas. Betjeman later clarified that 'we have allowed the nibbling destruction of commercial speculators to destroy whole districts of incomparably beautiful Georgian parts of towns like Cheltenham, Leamington, Bath, Bristol, Liverpool, Birmingham, Newcastle upon Tyne, Edinburgh, Margate, Brighton [and] Weymouth.'

These were dangerous times for lovers of nineteenth-century architecture, or indeed any architecture. By now, Betjeman's passion for buildings had gained him the unofficial position of 'people's campaigner'. He was also president of a growing number of conservation groups. The most important of these was the Victorian Society, which he formed in 1958 with his friend Anne Rosse, who lived at 18 Stafford Terrace in London. Her grandfather, the former *Punch* artist Linley Sambourne, had bought the house in 1874 and decorated it in contemporary style; Betjeman was one of the few who agreed that it should be protected. The Society aimed to save 'best Victorian buildings and their contents' and enjoyed the legal right to be consulted when the redevelopment or demolition of a Victorian building was being proposed.

Although he never lost his contempt for the peculiarly Victorian form of vandalism known as church restoration, Betjeman knew that Victorian architecture was unpopular among critics and historians and needed protecting more than most. In 1949 he decided it was time to 'speak up' in

17

The architect of St Mark's church, Swindon, was Sir George Gilbert Scott. Opened in 1845, it was built to serve the new community around the town's Great Western Railway works. Betjeman once claimed that St Mark's taught him not to judge churches 'only by their architecture'; he often looked beyond the textbook when he could see genuine faith and genuine people.

its favour. In a radio talk on St Mark's Church, Swindon, he announced that Victorian church architects could be 'as original and creative and beautiful as any who've built before or since'. Though he singled out G. E. Street's St John's, Torquay (1867), where the Gothic Revival was concerned, his favourite architect would always be J. N. Comper (1864–1960), whose Molesworth Chapel (in Little Petherick church) he had seen as a boy. As the years went by, the two became friends, the younger man going on (successfully) to campaign for the elder's knighthood. Comper impressed the poet with the idea that a church should 'bring you to your knees when you first enter it'. Betjeman in turn extolled Comper as 'the logical outcome of the Gothic Revival', who did for churches 'what Voysey [had done] for small houses'.

The poet would later assert that 'the chief objections to Victorian architecture' included the misapprehension that nineteenth-century building practice stood mainly for 'back-to-back houses', 'immoral' decoration (as on Tower Bridge) and a lack of planning. It was acceptable to admire the Crystal Palace, he went on, for being 'the first prefab'.

The engineering feats of Brunel, Stephenson and Barlow were also acceptable to critics, which was why Cubitt's King's Cross station 'was preferred in all its stark simplicity to the romantic outlines of Gilbert Scott's St Pancras Hotel'. All these objections were 'being overcome by time'; indeed, it is partly thanks to Betjeman's efforts in the 1960s to highlight the impending doom of Gilbert Scott's masterpiece that we are able to enjoy its splendour today.

By the middle of the twentieth century even Philip Morton Shand had started to worry that he might have helped create 'a monster' in the 1930s. 'Contemporary Architecture,' he wrote to Betjeman, '= the piling up of gigantic children's toy bricks in utterly dehumanized and meaningless forms'. It was 'no longer funny'; it was 'a frightening, all-invading menace'. Betjeman's answer to the problem was to continue to raise awareness of the issues. In the early 1970s, he did this in part by contributing regular columns to the *Sunday Express* and *Private Eye*. One '*Eye*' feature saw him 'thank' those he saw as responsible 'for destroying so many of the Georgian Squares and Terraces so long a notorious impediment to enlightened planning'. The *Weekend* magazine of the *Daily Telegraph* also carried his major series on building styles, which was later collected into the 1972 book *A Pictorial History of English Architecture*. The author hoped this lavishly illustrated volume would 'communicate enthusiasm' for buildings to a wide audience. In this, Betjeman was largely successful, but, as we shall see, even he would not win every fight against 'the new barbarism'.

Cubitt's elegant King's Cross station building of 1852, seen here with 1970s additions in 2010. Modernists were allowed to admire its clean, functional lines.

UNDERGROUND

BY DISTRICT RAILWAY.

RIGHT INTO THE HEART OF THE COUNTRY,

BOOK TO HARROW, SUDBURY OR PERIVALE.

St James' Park Station Offices, S.W.

Johnson, Riddle & Co Ltd London S.E.

SOUND OF THE SUBURBS

I N 1971 Betjeman wrote to the Controller of the BBC about an idea for a new television film. He wanted to present a vision of British suburbia, which he could lavish with 'praise and stimulation'. 'What trim gardens we could show,' he gushed, 'what shopping arcades, front halls, churches, schools and human-scale paths and bicycle tracks and open spaces.' The Controller agreed and the result became the quintessential Betjeman film, *Metro-land*.

The term 'Metro-land', as Betjeman explains in the film, was used by the Metropolitan Railway Company to describe the new housing estates that were built along its line from Baker Street in London to Middlesex, Hertfordshire and Buckinghamshire in the early years of the twentieth century. These were the days of swift electric trains and gleaming rails, and of the optimism with which Betjeman's poem 'The Metropolitan Railway – BAKER STREET STATION BUFFET' (1953) begins:

> Early Electric! With what radiant hope
> Men formed this many-branched electrolier,
> Twisted the flex around the iron rope
> And let the dazzling vacuum globes hang clear[.]

Betjeman loved fantasising about the sorts of people who lived in different types of houses. Suburbia, with its ever-twitching lace curtains, hiding all manner of snobberies and infidelities, seemed to lend itself to the creation of comic colonels from Camberley and bountiful maidens from Dorking or Aldershot. He was usually half in love with the things he mocked and claimed suburbs – along with mineral railways, garden cities and Gothic churches – to be part of his background. As he reveals in *Metro-land*, Marlborough Road station was once near the home of his 'future parents-in-law', while the Palace of Arts at Wembley was where he used to wait for his father, who would disappear to study 'the living models' in Pears' Palace of Beauty. *Metro-land* finds delight in the Neasden Nature Trail, Harrow School (which Betjeman always claimed to have attended 'in all but fact') and the splendid Venetian décor of the clubhouse at Moor Park

Opposite:
Though well served by the Met, in 1903 the Metropolitan District Railway (later the District Line) opened a branch from Park Royal & Twyford Abbey, through Sudbury, to a terminus at South Harrow. It was the first of the Underground's surface lines to be electrified and was extended to meet the Met at Rayners Lane in 1910, allowing District trains to run to Uxbridge. South Harrow is now part of the Piccadilly Line, which took over this section in 1932.

A postcard showing Metropolitan Railway no. 17, an electric locomotive of 1923 vintage. Locomotives of this type worked passenger trains on the Met until 1961. Later named *Florence Nightingale*, no. 17 was withdrawn from service in 1943 following an accident.

A postcard of semis in Station Road, Harrow, in the early years of the twentieth century. Some remain, although many have since been converted to shops.

Golf Club near Rickmansworth. Yet the 'younger, brighter, homelier Metro-land' of Wembley is not quite the paradise it seems: the house names – 'Rusholme', 'Rustles', 'Rusty Tiles', 'Rose Hill', 'Rose Mount', 'Rose Roof' – may sound poetic in isolation, but as a roll call the uniform lack of imagination is clear; thus, when Betjeman observes that these residences stand on fields 'that once were bright with buttercups', his tone is one of regret.

STATION ROAD, WEALDSTONE.

No one could blame anyone for wanting to escape the grime and bustle of the city, but in a 1963 newspaper article Betjeman had shown the other side of progress by mourning the lost paradise of rural Middlesex. 'Somewhere,' he wrote, 'if I dared to raise my eyes above the crowded pavement, there must have been sky, but between it and me were concrete lamp standards, the tops of buses and enormous lorries carrying mattresses, and bulk liquids, or dragging trailers full of chassis of motor-cars'; slowly, the county was being stripped of 'the richest agricultural land near London'. Transport played a large part in this 'invasion', first by the main-line railway and then by the 'Met'.

Metro-land continues this theme in Harrow. After showing a street of solid houses built in the 1880s or 1890s, the camera pans on to 'the Sunday morning rhythm', as lawns are mown and cars washed outside a later speculation, with its bow-fronted, two-storey 1920s semis — all half-timber and hydrangeas. 'Variety,' Betjeman wryly explains, is 'created in each façade of the houses — in the colouring of the trees.' Had the country really come to the suburbs?

The further from Baker Street Betjeman travels in the film, however, the lighter his censure becomes. After praise for Norman Shaw's Grim's Dyke (1870) – a house in Harrow Weald once owned by the dramatist and librettist W. S. Gilbert – Betjeman continues to Chorleywood. Here, the 'country quality' lived on; here, perhaps, it was still as rural as 'rural RAYNER'S LANE' (as he described it in 'The Metropolitan Railway'). Chorleywood also had the advantage of being the location of The Orchard (1899), home of C. F. A. Voysey, and itself 'the parent of thousands of simple English houses'.

Betjeman then visits Quainton Road station and notes how the Metropolitan had originally intended it to be another Clapham Junction (with links even to a proposed Channel tunnel). Alas, these elaborate schemes came to nothing. Journey's end is therefore the rural outpost of Verney Junction: a place the houses never reached. 'Grass triumphs,' he concludes, 'and I must say I'm rather glad.'

The need to highlight the loss of verdant pasture land was also behind Betjeman's most notorious poem – 'Slough' (1937):

> Come, friendly bombs, and fall on Slough
> It isn't fit for humans now,
> There isn't grass to graze a cow
> Swarm over, Death!

Some critics saw only snobbery here, for the emphasis is clearly not on the middle-class homes of Metro-land, but on those of 'ordinary people' (as one of them put it). In fact, Betjeman felt that the houses his downtrodden office

HIGH STREET, HARROW ON THE HILL

5

The High Street,
Harrow-on-the-
Hill, in the 1940s.

clerks had to live in were shoddy, like the 1920s villas of Harrow. In *A Pictorial History of English Architecture* (1972), he described Slough's 'bow-windowed two-storey houses', which had been badly constructed by speculative builders, who wanted to squeeze as much money from a site as possible by building 'as close together as the by-laws would allow (sometimes closer)'. In this sense, 'Slough' attacks those developers whose aim was 'not solidity or value for money, but an outward appearance that made it impossible for a visitor to mistake his products for council houses'. The Slough Trading Estate (as Betjeman reminded a correspondent in 1967) had also been built on 'some of the most valuable agricultural land in England'. This explains the reference to preparing for the plough at the end of the poem, which recalls William Morris's plea in *The Earthly Paradise* (1868–70) to 'Forget the snorting steam and piston stroke' of the 'hideous town'.

Later eyes might smile on the 1930s semis and the leafy avenues on which they stand, but Betjeman knew of the nobler philanthropy behind some of the earlier estates. In his article 'Suburbs Common or Garden' (1960), he had written that eighteenth-century thinking revolved around the 'extension of the town into the fields'; subsequent builders 'wanted to make country of towns' so that each resident had a house with its own garden. Newly enriched Victorians later extended the idea by building larger houses in areas such as Streatham

The Orchard,
Chorleywood,
Hertfordshire,
designed by
C. F. A. Voysey
for himself and
built in 1899.

(London) and Jesmond Dene (Newcastle upon Tyne). Here there were elegant gas lamps silhouetted against the sky, 'and possibly a lodge at the entrance, laurels along the drive (in which Sherlock Holmes might be hiding with his bull's-eye lantern), red paper in the dining room and heavy mahogany chairs'.

'Suburbs Common or Garden' also mentioned Bedford Park in Chiswick, which had been laid out by Norman Shaw in 1876. Betjeman described how its 'winding roads' had been 'cut through by heavy traffic', and how 'the fences so carefully designed as part of the whole composition' had become 'dilapidated or altered'. Just two years later Acton Council demolished The Bramptons, a large house in Bedford Road, and built a yellow-brick retirement home in its place. Betjeman had called the estate the 'most significant suburb built in the last [nineteenth] century, probably the most significant in the Western World'. This ensured that he became part of the struggle to stop further development.

Betjeman's benign attitude was also extended to Broomhill in Sheffield, 'where gabled black stone houses rise above the ponticums and holly and private cast-iron lamp-posts light the gravelled drives'. This was 'the prettiest suburb in England', and Betjeman used it to contrast with his description of the 'worn little houses' that the poor were forced to live in. The main problem comes, as in 'Slough', when things went too far. As he wrote in

The Vicarage on
the Bedford Park
estate, Chiswick,
as featured in
The Building News,
17 June 1881.
The architect
was E. J. May.

1952, 'England, though not yet so ugly as Northern France and Belgium, is
nearly so,' and suburbs 'which once seemed so lovely' have spread 'so far in
the wake of the motor car that there is little but suburb left.' He also feared
that people had become passive acceptors of mediocrity, whose indifference
was evident in the blandness of the growing consumer age. Significantly,
when 'the suburbanite leaves Wembley for Wells he finds that the High Street
there is just like home'.

Metro-land and poems like 'Middlesex' (1954) voice some of these
concerns, but the balance between attractive housing and the destruction of
the landscape is perhaps caught best in Betjeman's 1963 film *Swindon and
North Lew*. In Swindon, the place 'the railways made great', the focus falls on
the Railway Village – 'what must be the first garden city in the world' – which
the Great Western Railway had built for its new workforce in 1841.
Discussing how the town expanded, Betjeman critiques its post-war housing
estates. These, he says, are 'not haphazard growth' like the Swindon of old,
but are 'sudden and deliberate, like a bomb'. 'You wouldn't know you were
in Wiltshire,' he adds, as the camera pans round the new dwellings, 'you
wouldn't even know you were in Swindon.' The only good he can see in all
this is that the Old Town, high up on the hill, has become 'an oasis of quiet'.
This returns us to Verney Junction, and the ultimate sense of 'enough is
enough' with which *Metro-land* ends.

Opposite:
In 1841 the Great
Western Railway
built what
Betjeman
described as 'the
first garden city
in the world' for
those employed
in nearby Swindon
Works. They are
still known locally
as 'the Company's
houses'.

FOR THE LOVE OF RAILWAYS

BETJEMAN'S INTEREST in railways went beyond Metro-land – and indeed the Metropolitan Railway. He owned books on obscure branch lines, books on mineral railways, books of celebration and books by railway professionals. Although the passenger perspective would remain paramount, he felt that a stationmaster's life was 'something worth living' and saw the nobility of those who worked in the great locomotive factories and sheds of Britain. On BBC Radio's *Desert Island Discs* in 1975, the host, Roy Plomley, recognised that the poet's 'special love' of railways must have added a 'zest' to his travels. But, he went on, was that love just for steam or did it extend 'into the present day of Inter-City'? Betjeman answered that he liked both, but admitted that he was fond of the comfort afforded by modern British Rail (BR) trains. He had found the Manchester Pullman so comfortable two years before that he was able to draft his poem '14 November 1973' – which commemorates the marriage of HRH Princess Anne to Captain Mark Phillips – after four large whiskies 'slowly consumed' in his carriage.

When Betjeman was born, railways were in the ascendant and steam was the prime source of motive power. Trains had gone from representing a slightly scary vision of the future – and thief of valuable estate land – to being the most effective way of travelling the length and breadth of Britain. Thus getting to and from prep school in Oxford, college in Marlborough and university back in Oxford required the young John to take a Great Western service from London Paddington. Many Cornish holidays would have also begun on a crowded platform at Paddington, waiting for departure time amid cases, buckets, spades and raincoats. Later still, as a resident of Uffington and Wantage, Betjeman's familiarity grew as he headed to the capital to work on the *Architectural Review*, or for the BBC. Even today, West Country commuters' hearts are gladdened when the graffiti of the Metropolis are replaced by the lush green of Royal Berkshire.

This was the railway Betjeman celebrated in his introduction to George Perry's 1970 volume *The Book of the Great Western*, the 'copper-capped' company of Brunel, the broad gauge and, later, the celebrated 'Castle' and

Opposite: Betjeman loved the Great Western Railway for its 'personality', which was fostered by its strident publicity department, the dedicated staff of which was responsible for producing many books, guides and posters. This example was designed by Edward McKnight Kauffer in 1932 and shows a path lined with stone walls, enticing the passenger to follow it to the Cornish sea shore. McKnight Kauffer also designed the cover for Betjeman's second volume of poetry, *Continual Dew* (1937).

'King' class locomotives. In 'that sad year of 1923' (as he called it), some 120 railway companies were grouped into the famous 'Big Four' – the London Midland & Scottish (LMS), London & North Eastern (LNER), Southern (SR) and Great Western (GWR). While the LMS, LNER and SR were totally new concerns, the Great Western merely expanded and – importantly for Betjeman – retained its 'personality'. He often gave away his preference for the constituent predecessors of the other three, such as the Midland Railway and the Somerset & Dorset, whose liveries bore romantic names like 'crimson lake' and 'Prussian blue'. This held true even forty years on: in the film *John Betjeman Goes by Train* (1962), he can be seen delighting in the Great Eastern insignia on the station bench at Snettisham ('and by the way, it's called "Snetcham", though it's spelled "Snett-iss-ham"').

The extent of the rail network throughout much of the twentieth century was such that there were often several ways of travelling between two places. Betjeman took pleasure in planning unnecessarily complex journeys, using his trusty Bradshaw all-line timetable. And, of course, there was another way to Cornwall – via the London & South Western from Waterloo, the final leg of which – over the River Camel – he once described as the most beautiful stretch of line he knew. After the 1923 Grouping, the Southern Railway took over these services and, from 1926, introduced the 'Atlantic Coast Express', whose carriages would be uncoupled en route and taken on to Ilfracombe, Seaton, Sidmouth, Exmouth and Padstow by a series of engines, while the

An original 1920s postcard, showing the 'Atlantic Coast Express' in the charge of steam locomotive no. 850 *Lord Nelson*, the doyen of a class introduced by the Southern Railway in 1926.

rest of the train continued behind another, often larger, locomotive to Plymouth. The Southern was also a pioneer of electric traction, its London suburban network being fully switched on in 1929, with a new service to Brighton following four years later. *This* Southern was the one featured in the poem 'Love in a Valley' (1937) – the one whose 'living' rails took young lovers to secret trysting places and homesteads hidden by pine trees.

Betjeman frequently reminded readers (or viewers, or listeners) where beauty was to be found 'just up the road'. The Second World War had lent an urgency to this message, which became more potent when he was 'exiled' in Ireland as the United Kingdom's Press Attaché. He would continue to draw attention to architecture, the landscape and why they were important when the threat changed from bomber to developer. But though Betjeman had a love for fast driving – and had even been fined for speeding while researching the *Shell Guides* (a series itself designed to encourage automobile use) – he was no lover of cars per se and would come to see the perils of increasing motor traffic levels. He also knew that travelling by train offered a much better way of enjoying 'Unmitigated England', with its gabled farms and shimmering lakes, than travelling by road. Indeed, donning his mac and Pickwick hat for the television film *Branch Line Railway* in 1963, he urged viewers to 'Forget motor-cars, get rid of anxiety,' adding from his carriage that it was nice to see Glastonbury Tor 'without a foreground of villas and petrol stations' (which is how one sees it from a car or coach). Sadly, this possibility was soon to be destroyed by Dr Beeching.

Richard Beeching was brought in by the government to run BR in 1961. His remit was to make the railways profitable. He presented his ideas in his famous report, *The Reshaping of British Railways*, which was published two years later. Although more than 3,000 miles of 'unremunerative' lines had already been closed, Beeching's plan to close 6,000 miles more drew much attention from the press, which dubbed it the 'Beeching Axe'. Controversy came with some of the Doctor's choices, many of which, like the Glastonbury branch, but also the main Somerset & Dorset route from Bath to Bournemouth and the Great Central from Sheffield to London Marylebone, were beloved by enthusiasts and romantics alike. A number of 'last rites' ceremonies were carried out, with wreaths tied to smokebox doors and pall-bearers carrying coffins of memories on trains across the country. It is wrong to dismiss Beeching as malevolent, but the 'Axe' was difficult to ignore. Betjeman's attitude to the value of the rail network was clear in *Branch Line Railway*, as were his fears for those who would lose their jobs when lines were closed. He lent his support to many rail preservation campaigns and used poems like 'Dilton Marsh Halt' (1968) to help raise awareness.

In a 1953 radio broadcast, Betjeman had described the beauty of the railways and claimed that many lines were 'as much a part of the beauty of

England as Compton Wynyates' in Warwickshire. For him, beauty was to be found not only at the front of the train: it was there too in the viaducts, the bridges and the stations – from the dark-platformed cathedrals of steam in cities to the 'rectory' styles on rural branch lines, where geraniums climbed white stucco walls and stationmasters' cats languished on long summer afternoons. One of his favourites was Aldersgate Street, opened by the 'Met' in 1865, and whose buffet once specialised in afternoon tea. Much like the GWR, this oasis of Earl Grey had remained a 'memorial to unwilling co-operation' after the amalgamation of several independent Underground lines and their eventual take-over by the London Passenger Transport Board (later London Transport) in 1933. Aldersgate Street was sadly bombed during the Second World War and its fine overall roof was demolished in 1955. Betjeman captured the scene, and the mood, in verse:

> Snow falls in the buffet of Aldersgate station,
> Toiling and doomed from Moorgate Street puffs the train,
> For us of the steam and the gas-light, the lost generation,
> The new white cliffs of the City are built in vain.

Opposite, top:
A Metropolitan
Railway ticket from
Aldersgate Street
to Bishopsgate;
the fare (third
class) was just 1d.

Left: The delightful
station at Barnack,
on the Great
Northern line
between Stamford
and Wansford.
The line was
closed by the
London & North
Eastern Railway
in 1929.

Betjeman's architectural conservationism began to grow during this period. One of his most famous campaigns concerned Philip Hardwick's grand Doric Arch at Euston, built for the London & Birmingham Railway in 1837. This was due to be flattened when a new terminus was built as part of BR's West Coast Main Line electrification scheme. To rally support, Betjeman wrote an article for the *Daily Telegraph*. He could, he said, think of 'no worthier memorial to the fact that Britain built the first railways' than to reconstruct the Arch on Euston Road. This had been the part of the original plan, but,

Detail from an
original London &
North Western
Railway postcard
of Hardwick's
magnificent Doric
Arch at Euston,
1904.

despite the efforts of the Georgian Group and the Victorian Society, it was soon scrapped. Demolition began in December 1961.

The modern, concrete Euston failed to rouse Betjeman's passions. He dismissed it as 'no masterpiece' and said that its lack of platform seating made it an 'inhuman' place, which seemed 'to ignore passengers'. Thankfully, he was to have better luck with helping beat BR's plan to combine St Pancras and King's Cross by bulldozing most of the former and all of the latter. Betjeman joined forces with the Victorian Society in opposition. A 1967 application for a Grade I listing for both W. H. Barlow's train shed at St Pancras and Sir George Gilbert Scott's magnificent hotel was successful; the station was secure and went on to be reborn in 2007 as an international terminus for the Channel Tunnel. Fittingly, it was also the site of Betjeman's last public appearance. A suggestion to the Chairman of BR, Sir Peter Parker, led to a short ceremony at the terminus on 24 June 1983. After a speech and the swish of a curtain, newly named locomotive 86229 *Sir John Betjeman* hauled a train of enthusiasts northward while Poet Laureate Sir John Betjeman took lunch in nearby Euston House, where he was presented with a model of the Euston Arch.

The irony was not lost on him.

Opposite:
Sir George Gilbert Scott's St Pancras station hotel of 1868, seen after restoration work in the early twenty-first century.

Betjeman with Sir Peter Parker (right) at St Pancras on 24 June 1983, in order to name locomotive no. 86229 after the poet. It was to be Betjeman's last public appearance.

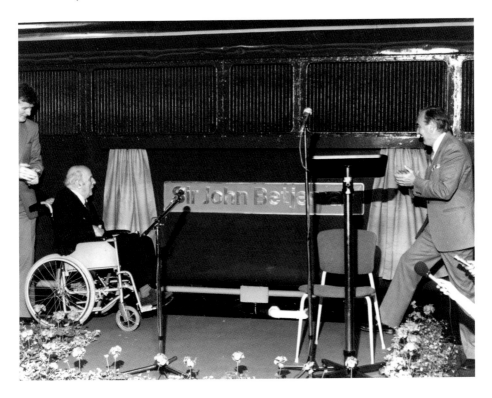

BETJEMAN AND CORNWALL

THE RAILWAYS Betjeman loved were shaped by a Cornishman. In 1804 an engineer from Illogan – Richard Trevithick – built the first locomotive, a four-wheeled steam engine for the Pen-y-Darren Ironworks in Merthyr Tydfil, South Wales. From its success came other famous engines, such as *Puffing Billy* and *Rocket*, and from them grew a golden age. Just fifty-five years after Trevithick's first step, the last span of Isambard Kingdom Brunel's Royal Albert Bridge was lifted into place, allowing trains to pass over the River Tamar from Devon into Cornwall for the first time. Though hugely beneficial to local industry, by the twentieth century the railways had also started to open the county to holidaymakers. Many of the wealthier ones rented cottages for a restful summer, taking in the healthy sea air.

Ernest and Bess Betjemann began following this path before their son was born. The couple would take a train, travelling through the London suburbs, out into the Home Counties and on towards Dartmoor and the Duchy. They favoured the quiet village of Trebetherick on the north coast, where the air was often more 'bracing' than 'healthy'. Here, Ernest could indulge his passions for shooting and golf, while Bess could read novels in peace. At first, they stayed at a boarding house, but Ernest soon decided to make his mark and have a house built in Trebetherick. 'Undertown' was a whitewashed Arts and Crafts affair in the Voysey manner, designed by Robert Atkinson, the architect of the Barber Institute of Fine Arts in Birmingham.

'Childhood,' as Betjeman wrote in *Summoned by Bells*, 'is measured out in sounds and smells / And sights, before the dark of reason grows.' And he certainly found the north coast of Cornwall a delight for the senses. From the refreshing ozone spray of the sea and the crashing of its waves, to the wreck of the *Angèle* on Doom Bar, it had a barren beauty of its own. Young John was destined to make many friends in this poet's land of lugworm casts, feathery tamarisks and forgotten cliff-paths; but he could also be by himself, and often chose to spend his days planning dams and castles in the sand or going on bike rides to explore lanes that could only be found on a one-inch map.

Later, during adolescence, these trips would evolve into the art of 'church crawling' – and there were plenty to crawl, Cornwall being awash with Celtic saints and the Methodism of John Wesley, who had visited the county thirty-two times between 1743 and 1787. Betjeman would tour the landscape, discovering nearby Rock, Tregardock, Port Isaac and St Endellion. He later described Blisland's church of St Protus and St Hyacinth as seeming 'to lean this way and that', throwing 'chapels and aisles in all directions'. By the time he first saw it, the Norman nave had been joined by a fifteenth-century tower, porch and transepts, all of which had been subject to 'restoration' in the Victorian era. It was a mixture of styles, but, as he said, 'what do dates and styles matter in Blisland church?' It was the 'real thing', bringing visitors to their knees as soon as they entered, which is how Betjeman's architectural hero Ninian Comper measured the true value of a place of worship.

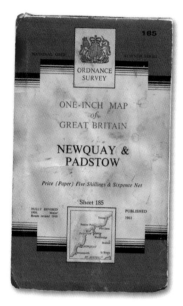

With the aid of a one-inch map much like this one, Betjeman explored the forgotten byways of Cornwall and, indeed, the Church of England.

The incoming tide on Daymer Beach, near Trebetherick, much as it looked during Betjeman's childhood.

27 The Incoming Tide on Daymer Beach

Port Isaac, Cornwall, in 1906. Betjeman wrote in 1952 that 'Port Isaac is Polperro without the self-consciousness, St Ives without the artists'. He would recognise it still.

Another cycling tour took Betjeman to St Ervan, whose priest lent him a copy of Arthur Machen's schoolboy novel *The Secret Glory* (1922). The book seemed to reflect the young seeker's own life and needs, portraying as it does a callow, aesthetically minded youth with an interest in architecture, who finds comfort in the church. Reading it increased Betjeman's need to seek religious experiences all over Cornwall. One could argue that it was to be a lifelong journey. In *Summoned by Bells*, he describes how he then visited the local holy well and knelt down in the dark of St Enodoc, a church nestled in the sand dunes east of Daymer Bay. So well nestled was it in the eighteenth century that the parson had to be lowered through the roof in order to conduct the services required to earn his stipend. When the architect J. P. St Aubyn set about restoring it in the middle of the following century, it was also excavated. The adjacent golf course was opened soon after, in 1890. This post-excavation St Enodoc was the one Betjeman knew, the one in whose churchyard he was destined to be buried, and the one he celebrated in verse (*cf.* 'Sunday Afternoon Service in St Enodoc Church, Cornwall', 1944).

When Betjeman conceived the *Shell Guides* in 1932, there was really only one county with which he could begin. *Cornwall* was published two years later. Spiral-bound like an exercise book, it suffers a little from the 'Hastings effect' (being written while Betjeman was still working for the '*Archie Rev*'), and also from having the information on towns and churches printed in separate, jargon-heavy sections. Yet it sold well and would soon be joined by poems about the sea and childhood, and by radio broadcasts extolling the virtues of the county and its traditions (like the famous Padstow 'Obby 'Oss spring festival). The entirely rewritten second edition (1964) was much more Betjeman than Hastings, which arguably made Cornwall even more attractive to its readers. The entry on Callington illustrates the bittersweet irony its author felt at having helped encourage visitors: 'Just below the church a fine Georgian house front has been murdered by the modernistic extension of a shop. The inhabitants of the town have mostly moved into bungalows and council estates on the outskirts.' A later poem, 'Delectable Duchy' (1974), further laments the shattering of peace by developers and tourists, in similar fashion to Betjeman's yearning for the Middlesex lost to Metro-land. For him, the discarded crisp packets and broken toys which had started to litter the beaches represented the growth of what he called 'Trebenidorm', with its whitewashed, flat-roofed holiday homes and caravans.

Cornwall's economy now depends on tourism, but for Betjeman it remained a safe haven – one to which he returned year after year. In 1959 he bought Treen House in Trebetherick and it was here that he would come to spend his last days.

Betjeman's final resting place: the church of St Enodoc, near Trebetherick, which dates back to the fifteenth century. As part of the building's Victorian restoration, it had to be dug out of the sand that had gradually encroached upon it.

FAITH AND DOUBT

FOR A BRIEF MOMENT at Marlborough College, John Betjeman – the self-confessed 'religious maniac' – stared into the void and flirted with atheism. 'Give me a God whom I can touch and see,' as he pleaded from the college chapel in *Summoned by Bells*. The institutionalised portrayals of God found in public schools did little to inspire him, but those Cornish summer holidays certainly did – especially after he had read the copy of Machen's *The Secret Glory* lent to him by the priest of St Ervan. From here, Betjeman developed into a staunch Anglo-Catholic, who wrote poems (notably 'In a Bath Teashop', 1945) in which the theologian H. A. Williams could perceive the Divine Charity. And yet there was a time when it was uncertain whose bells would ultimately summon him.

Surprisingly, during the 1930s Betjeman became a member of the Religious Society of Friends. His interest may have been roused by the historian and philosopher Gerald Heard, who believed the Society to be a positive force for Christian revival. Betjeman was attending Quaker meetings by the early part of 1929 but did not become a formal member until 1931. His spiritual journey was clearly continuing, yet the fact that he waited two years before joining seems more like a toe being dipped into water than anything more devout.

Indeed, all evidence indicates that his membership was fairly unremarkable: while a Quaker, he raised no concerns, sat on no committees, and warranted no official Quaker presence at his wedding in 1933. Neither did membership bring about an increase in sober piety: it was during this period, after all, that he spent most weekends with rich friends at huge country houses, and wavered romantically between several women while enjoying their lavish hospitality. He even proposed to one of them during his engagement. However, the interlude does seem to have affected Betjeman's contemporary poetry. While references to puritan Sandemanians, Baptists, Wesleyans and so on tally with a man who delighted in the obscure byways of English Protestantism, his tone is often satirical. 'The Sandemanian Meeting-House in Highbury Quadrant' (1931), for example, shows with

Opposite:
A mid-period photograph of John Betjeman. By this time, the poet's flirtation with Quakerism was behind him, and the Anglo-Catholicism for which he is remembered was well established.

some significance how the old Sandemanians are 'hidden from the sun', while 'An Eighteenth Century Calvinistic Hymn' (1931) sends up the dour fire-and-brimstone preachers once associated with this creed, the like of whom would have struck terror into the hearts of small children.

Discussing the Welsh poet R. S. Thomas in 1955, Betjeman noted

Marlborough College's chapel became a haven of peace and contemplation for the young Betjeman, but religious doubt would dog him for most of his life.

The beautiful Norman abbey at Wymondham, Norfolk, in which Sir Ninian Comper's gold reredos may be found.

that many 'good Welsh writers' had been 'driven to satire and contempt by the narrow Calvinism of mercenary peasantry'; moreover, 'Poor Morgan' (of Thomas's 'The Minister' – 'well versed' in the said theology) did not trust beauty in the landscape or in women – hardly Betjemanian traits! In a 1946 radio broadcast, Betjeman had revealed his love for Calvinist clergyman Augustus Montague Toplady, writer of hymns like 'Rock of Ages' and 'A Debtor to Mercy Alone'. But, though violently uncompromising in his views, Toplady was a skilful essayist, whose prose was a joy to read; he was also charming and blessed with a ready wit. Betjeman's Calvinist childhood nursemaid possessed none of these qualities, but it was from her that he caught his fear of endlessness. Sadly, this would have more lasting significance.

By the time *Continual Dew* was published in 1937, Betjeman had left the Quakers and had returned to type, becoming People's Warden at St Mary's church in Uffington (then in Berkshire, now Oxfordshire), to where he and his family had moved in 1934. Much of his subsequent prose writing and a number of his broadcasts praised church architecture. Comper remained a favourite practitioner, featuring in Betjeman's earliest work right up to the BBC television programme *A Passion for Churches* in 1974, in which he praised the 'lofty reredos of sculptured gold' Comper had made for Wymondham's Norman abbey in Norfolk.

This film begins with Betjeman rowing a small boat on the River Bure in Norfolk. As he nears Belaugh, he looks across to the tower of St Peter's and recalls enjoying the same view during childhood. It was this, he says, which gave him his 'passion for churches', 'so that every church I've been past since, I've wanted to stop and look in.' For Betjeman, churches embellished the landscape and imbued it with a beauty that no railway station or well-designed villa could ever match. The younger man's aesthetic sense was often offended by heavy-handed Victorian church restoration. While the older man retained this distaste, he made exceptions where faith overcame the architectural schism (as at Blisland in Cornwall) – although such tolerance never seemed to extend to modern additions like electric lighting. In 'Before the Anaesthetic or A Real Fright' (1945), he showed that he appreciated the danger of letting eye and ear outrank the soul, by admitting that his obsession with church-crawling may have been more façade than faith at times.

The interior of St John the Baptist's church, Lound, Suffolk. Comper added gold to the font cover (to 'emphasise the sacrament of baptism') and to the screen ('to veil the mystery of holy communion at the high altar').

St Peter's, Belaugh, Norfolk. This view – or one very like it – gave Betjeman his 'passion for churches'.

For one who delighted in humour, Betjeman claimed that death is perhaps the only thing that gives life a sense of proportion. The fear instilled by his Calvinist nursemaid would return to haunt him, and the sense of doubt that went with it would find a voice in poems like 'For Nineteenth-Century Burials' (1931), which seems to challenge the ability of religion to offer succour, 'Christmas' (1947), which repeatedly asks 'And is it true?', and 'Loneliness' (1971), in which it seems as though life is preparing to carry on as normal, without Betjeman, before his very eyes.

Betjeman's wife Penelope had also been blighted by doubt in the mid-1940s. She chose to seek solace in Roman Catholicism – a move that helped speed the end of her marriage. She and John never divorced, but he would soon seek rooms of his own in London and was never able to reconcile himself to the 'empty pew' beside him in his local Anglican church. In his poetry, he would comment that the differences between Protestantism and Catholicism seem unimportant 'in the face of death' (cf. 'Remorse', 1953). Like all good debaters, however, he also explored the ways belief could overcome uncertainty, as in 'Saint Cadoc' (1940), where the fear of war is tempered by a mixture of faith and the comfort offered by the Cornish coastline:

> [D]eath is now the gentle shore
> With Land upon the cliffs before
> And in his cell beside the sea
> The Celtic saint has prayed for me.

Despite such optimism, Death and its consorts, Faith and Doubt, would continue to provide a nip in the air into the 1970s. By this time, Betjeman was starting to suffer from Parkinson's disease, a debilitating illness that leaves its sufferers physically unable to do what their minds continue to desire. When his final volume of new verse was published in 1974, he would have known that, while not yet at death's door, Parkinson's was placing his hand on the handle sooner than the average man could expect. This led to musings like those found in 'On Leaving Wantage 1972', where the clashing bells convey a coldness which suggests that Betjeman does not expect to dance to the music of time like the novelist Anthony Powell, but drown in its waters.

By the end of his life, Betjeman's fear had started to diminish. This was due in part to the peace of mind afforded by his long-term relationship with

Lady Elizabeth Cavendish, a lady-in-waiting to Princess Margaret and member of the Devonshire family, whom he had met in 1951. 'I used to think death was some fearful jab of pain,' he told documentary film-maker Jonathan Stedall in 1982. Now, he was not so certain 'that it's not with us all the time'. Stedall quotes H. A. Williams's belief that death is simply 'letting go'. Betjeman agrees, but when asked if he has any regrets, sidesteps by remarking famously: 'I haven't had enough sex.'

The last laugh remained his.

The peal of ten bells at Christ Church, Swindon, was celebrated in verse by Betjeman in 1945. In the busy, industrialised town the bells struggle to be heard, but heard they certainly are.

BETJEMAN THE LAUREATE

THE POSITION of Poet Laureate was created by James I for Ben Jonson in 1617, although it did not become a formal honour until conferred on John Dryden in 1670. Among the most famous Poets Laureate are William Wordsworth (from 1843 to 1850) and Alfred, Lord Tennyson (1850–92). Robert Southey is usually considered the first modern one, as it was he (from 1813) who began to steer the role away from the monarchy towards the life of the nation. It remains a difficult job: to some, those who accept it are puppets of the establishment; others are disappointed if the high standard they have set for the incumbent is not attained. Payment has varied down the years, but alcohol is usually included, perhaps in recognition of its relationship with inspiration. Most recently, the reward has included a 'butt of sack', which is roughly equivalent to 100 gallons of sherry.

Betjeman was appointed Poet Laureate in Ordinary to Her Majesty Queen Elizabeth II on 10 October 1972, succeeding his friend Cecil Day-Lewis, who had died that May. It was hard to deny the sense of inevitability: from around 1940, Betjeman's poetry had started to express recognisable truths about contemporary Britain; he had also produced a few royal poems already, including a light-hearted, extemporised piece on the birth of Prince Andrew in February 1960, and a 'Poem for Princess Margaret's Wedding Day' later the same year. His first one, however ('Death of King George V'), had appeared back in 1937. With its references to a well-documented love of pheasant shoots and philately, it captures the essence of the Sailor King perfectly. The poem also illustrates the watershed between the old world of men who 'never cheated' and the new world of 'red suburbs', indicated most profoundly by the fact that George V is borne skywards by birds, while (in the last line) his successor comes back to earth by aeroplane.

More recently, the now-knighted Betjeman had written 'A Ballad of the Investiture, 1969'. As the poem clarifies, HRH Prince Charles had specifically asked him to produce the piece; the request is jokingly referred to as a 'command', but Sir John left the task undone for several years, publication coming some five years after the event. Not wishing to tread on the toes of

Opposite:
In 1954 Betjeman began renting rooms in Cloth Fair, near Smithfield Market, partly to give himself a London base for broadcasting and journalism. By 1973 the noise from the delivery lorries had become so great that he was forced to move. He found accommodation in Radnor Walk, Chelsea. Here, he is reading proofs of Gavin Stamp's book *Temples of Power* in September 1979.

a friend was part of it (Cecil Day-Lewis was still Poet Laureate at the time); fear and self-doubt made up the rest. Nervousness is certainly imparted in some of the early lines, but ultimately the poem works because, though public, it is addressed privately to the Prince:

> You know those moments that there are
> When, lonely under moon and star,
> You wait upon a beach?
> Suddenly all Creation's near
> And complicated things are clear,
> Eternity in reach!

Betjeman later cited Tennyson's 'The Charge of the Light Brigade' and 'Ode on the Death of the Duke of Wellington' (both 1855) as being among the best of any state verses written by a Laureate. There is perhaps a touch of the Tennysonian ability to set a scene in the opening of Betjeman's first official Laureate piece, which commemorates the marriage of HRH Princess Anne to Captain Mark Phillips on 14 November 1973 and begins with a fanfare of bells and birdsong as the bride and groom take their vows. To lubricate the flow of his pen, Betjeman turned not to his butt of sack, but to four double Scotches supped slowly on the train from Manchester to London. He wrote to the Queen's private secretary that he hoped the result was not too similar to 'Christmas card verse'. Many felt he was wrong: one Member of Parliament was apparently so appalled that he called for Betjeman's resignation.

The trouble was that Betjeman found it hard to write 'to order', having always equated poetry with freedom – something that Laureate verse rarely has anything to do with. Even Tennyson sometimes had trouble, as a glance at his 'Opening of the Indian and Colonial Exhibition by the Queen' (1885) will prove. Talking to Kingsley Amis in 1972, Betjeman recalled how John Masefield (in his view unsuccessfully) had compelled himself to write royal verse, adding simply that 'you can't force something that has to be inspired'. Other poems that featured in Betjeman's last collection (*A Nip in the Air*, 1974) were arguably more successful. One, 'Inland Waterway', had been read by its composer at the opening ceremony of the Upper Avon at Stratford in 1974. Its pace is sedate and peaceful, and the poet is clearly relishing the scene, with its slow-swinging lock gates and softly swaying barges. Such tranquillity was innately critical of the speed and greed of contemporary society, but 'Inland Waterway' also ends with the notion that in this river (and

THE ROYAL WEDDING : LONDON : 14th NOVEMBER 1973
H.R.H. Princess Anne and Captain Mark Phillips

COLLECTORCARD   C5002
Croydon CR0 1HW

so in all rivers, and perhaps all similar idylls) lies 'the heart of England'. There is a sense that Betjeman felt it was not too late to return to this pastoral state, although the final poem in the book, 'The Last Laugh', suggests that he thought he might not be around to witness it:

> I made hay while the sun shone.
>> My work sold.
> Now, if the harvest is over
>> And the world cold,
> Give me the bonus of laughter
>> As I lose hold.

A postcard which, like Betjeman's first Laureate poem, commemorates HRH Princess Anne's wedding to Captain Mark Phillips on 14 November 1973.

While Betjeman would live for another decade, his poetic harvest was indeed almost over. In May 1976, Prince Charles asked him for one of his 'masterpieces of scansion' to commemorate the Queen's Silver Jubilee the following year. He tried his best, but sensed that his effort had something of the jingle about it (although it was at least meant to be sung, not pondered over on a page). Malcolm Williamson, the Master of the Queen's Musick, heartened him by saying that the words left exactly the gaps he needed for his arrangement.

If Betjeman found the writing of patriotic poetry difficult, it was clear that the problem did not extend to other media. This was the era of some of his best television programmes, like *Metro-land* and *Betjeman in Australia*, the latter seeing him relish the trams of Bendigo, the Botanic Gardens of Melbourne and St John's Cathedral, Brisbane, which had been designed by John Loughborough Pearson, architect of Truro Cathedral in Cornwall. In *A Passion for Churches*, screened in 1974, he visited Norfolk to celebrate the Anglican Church and its places of worship. Watch it, and it is clear that it might as well have been called *A Passion for England*. Among various radio programmes, Betjeman made a superb series on hymns and poetry called *Sweet Songs of Zion* (1976–8), and also became a recording artist, releasing four long-playing albums of his poetry set to the music of Jim Parker. The beauty of these records is that Betjeman performs his work naturally – as only he could – to his own innate rhythm, while Parker's musical themes wash sympathetically (and highly effectively) around them. The initial result – released as *Betjeman's Banana Blush* in 1974 – was a great success and brought his work to a new audience. By now, his Parkinson's disease was more widely known, but it was mainly due to his studio work – coupled with the huge number of letters that he received each day (most of which he kindly answered) – that his prose output dropped during this period. Nevertheless, he still found time to write reviews and, in 1976, a piece for Margaret Drabble's *The Genius of Thomas Hardy*, in which he concentrated on Hardy's architectural apprenticeship.

Betjeman suffered a heart attack in 1978, yet his recovery was such that he managed to produce almost as much work as he had the year before. However, his failure to write a lament for the death of the popular Earl Mountbatten in 1979 did not go unnoticed, *Private Eye* (for one) quickly producing a parody. But while the poem he composed for the eightieth birthday of the Queen Mother (1980) was not his finest, the descriptively titled 'Ode on the Marriage of HRH Prince Charles to the Lady Diana Spencer in St Paul's Cathedral on 29 July 1981' was the best Laureate lyric he had produced for some years. Once again, this is partly because it addresses the couple personally:

> Blackbirds in City churchyards hail the dawn,
> Charles and Diana, on your wedding morn.
> Come College youths, release your twelve-voiced power
> Concealed within the graceful belfry tower…

Following the surprise discovery of a number of earlier (discarded) works, John Murray published *Uncollected Poems* in 1982. As Betjeman said himself, there may be 'a good line somewhere,' but 'I think I was quite right to reject this or that'. *Time with Betjeman* – the television series in which this view was aired – drew together clips from its subject's television films, interspersing them with contemporary interviews. Betjeman was now wheelchair-bound and clearly very frail, but his mind remained delightfully sharp: in one programme, he recites Tennyson's 'Northern Farmer, New Style' (1869) in a perfect Yorkshire accent, along with Philip Larkin's 'This Be the Verse' (1974), with eyes asparkle as he sounds the poem's famous expletives.

A couple of verses – 'Honest Doubts' and 'Anniversary Comment' – appeared in 1983. There could have been more, but in the September of that year Betjeman suffered another heart attack and, the following month, another stroke. Friends would visit and read to him at his London home, but Cornwall soon started to call.

Sir John made his final journey to Trebetherick in May 1984, passing peacefully away on the 19th in the company of his loved ones. The funeral took place a few days later at St Enodoc. Under a sympathetically stormy sky, the hearse stopped where the road ran out, 300 yards from the church; six pall-bearers carried the coffin slowly across the links, up the winding path and through the lych-gate. Betjeman left behind many friends, such as

Betjeman was responsible for saving St Pancras from demolition in the 1960s. When the station was closed for restoration and remodelling, Martin Jennings created an 8½-foot sculpture to celebrate the man and his work. It was unveiled on 12 November 2007 and stands at platform level.

Kingsley Amis, the journalist Simon Jenkins and the Australian comedian Barry Humphries. With them he had shared laughs, kindness, passions, poetry, art and song – much as he had with his readers, viewers and listeners. Such intimacy, honesty and enthusiasm is what made publicans, taxi drivers, doctors, night-club owners, subalterns and shop assistants mourn for him. Thankfully, his work lives on.

John Betjeman's grave at St Enodoc.

PLACES TO VISIT

Betjeman Memorial Park, near the Church of St Peter and St Paul, Church Street, Wantage, Oxfordshire OX12 8AQ.

Buckinghamshire Railway Centre, Quainton Road Station, Quainton, near Aylesbury, Buckinghamshire HP22 4BY.
Telephone: 01296 655720.
Website: www.bucksrailcentre.org

Highgate Literary and Scientific Institution, 11 South Grove, Highgate, London N6 6BS.
Telephone: 020 8340 3343.
Website: www.hlsi.net
Portrait of Sir John on permanent display.

St Enodoc Church, Trebetherick, Cornwall PL27 6SA. Betjeman's final resting place.

St Pancras International Railway Station, King's Cross Road, London WC1X 9DE. Commemorative statue and Betjeman Arms pub.

The Sir John Betjeman Centre, Southern Way, Wadebridge, Cornwall PL27 7BX.
Website: www.johnbetjeman.org.uk
Located in the former Wadebridge railway station; includes Betjeman memorabilia room.

Tom Brown's School Museum, Broad Street, Uffington, Oxfordshire SN7 7RA.
Website: www.museum.uffington.net
Includes Betjeman display.

FURTHER READING

BY JOHN BETJEMAN

Ghastly Good Taste, or a depressing story of the rise and fall of English architecture. Chapman & Hall, 1933.

First and Last Loves. John Murray, 1952. Betjeman's first prose collection, chosen by Myfanwy Piper, who was also celebrated in two 'golden' poems.

Collins Guide to English Parish Churches. Collins, 1958.

Summoned by Bells. John Murray, 1960. Betjeman's verse-autobiography.

London's Historic Railway Stations. John Murray, 1972.

A Pictorial History of English Architecture. John Murray, 1972. Excellent overview of the subject derived from Betjeman's series on architecture for the *Daily Telegraph Magazine*.

John Betjeman – Letters Volume One: 1926–1951; edited by Candida Lycett Green. Methuen, 1994.

John Betjeman – Letters Volume Two: 1951–1984; edited by Candida Lycett

Green. Methuen, 1995.

John Betjeman: Coming Home – An Anthology of Prose; edited by Candida Lycett Green. Methuen, 1997.

Collected Poems. John Murray, fifth edition 2006.

Trains and Buttered Toast: Selected Radio Talks; edited by Stephen Games. John Murray, 2006.

Sweet Songs of Zion; edited by Stephen Games. John Murray, 2007. Scripts from Betjeman's 1970s radio series on the poetry of hymns.

Tennis Whites and Teacakes; edited by Stephen Games. John Murray, 2008. Thematic selection of poetry, prose, radio and television scripts.

Betjeman's England; edited by Stephen Games. John Murray, 2009. Edited scripts from some of Betjeman's vast television output.

ABOUT JOHN BETJEMAN

Brown, Dennis. *Writers and Their Work: John Betjeman*. Northcote House, 1999. The first critical text to treat *Summoned by Bells* with the respect it deserves.

Gammond, Peter. *A Little Book of Betjeman*. Guidon Publishing, 2006.

Gardner, Kevin. *Betjeman and the Anglican Imagination*. SPCK, 2010. Looks at the highly important question of religion and its relationship with Betjeman and his work.

Heald, John (editor). *Remembering Sir John*. The Betjeman Society, 2006.

Hillier, Bevis. *John Betjeman: A Life in Pictures*. John Murray, 1984.

Hillier, Bevis. *Young Betjeman*. John Murray, 1988.

Hillier, Bevis. *John Betjeman: New Fame, New Love*. John Murray, 2002.

Hillier, Bevis. *Betjeman: The Bonus of Laughter*. John Murray, 2004. These four volumes by Hillier make up an important body of biographical information on Betjeman.

Morse, Greg. *John Betjeman: Reading the Victorians*. Sussex Academic Press, 2008. Examines the influence of Victorian culture and literature on Betjeman's poetry, prose and broadcasts.

Payton, Philip. *John Betjeman and Cornwall*. University of Exeter Press, 2010. Re-assesses the poet's lifelong relationship with his adopted county.

Wilson, A. N. *Betjeman*. Hutchinson, 2006. Shorter biography with emphasis on Betjeman's personal relationships.

Readers may also be interested in The Betjeman Society, which was founded to promote the study and appreciation of the life and work of Sir John Betjeman. Contact the Membership Secretary for details: 386 Hurst Road, Bexley, Kent DA5 3JY. (Website: www.johnbetjeman.com/society.html)

INDEX

Page numbers in italics refer to illustrations